Introduction

WE MAY, AS PET LOVERS, prefer cats in terms of sheer numbers, but there's no doubt we dote on our dogs more and have meddled with them more, too. From an animal that started out eating the scraps and trash from our ancestors' encampments, we've developed a companion animal and workmate that is so diverse and versatile it's difficult to imagine all dogs are really the same species.

But they are. Science tells us that doggy DNA is basically the same from Maltese to Mastiff, from Basset Hound to Greyhound. We have dogs who sniff out drugs and bombs, detect seizures and cancer, elevate moods and decrease blood pressure, herd sheep, retrieve birds, guard our stuff, help wheelchair users, pull sleds, and more — but most dogs these days just sleep on the couch. Born retired, if you will. The evolution of *canis lupus familiaris* from the wolfish animals of our ancestors to the stylish accessory pup in a celebrity's pricey handbag has been dramatic, and yet there's still plenty even the most ardent dog lover will find surprising about the animal who has for generations been man's (and woman's) best friend.

And that's what this book is all about — finding those entertaining tidbits to make you smile, raise an eyebrow in surprise, and most of all, learn something new that will help you to love your dog even more, no matter what size, shape, or mix of dog you love.

The dog is perhaps the only animal who understands and shares that most basic of human

Curiously Compelling Facts, True Tales, & Trivia Even Your Dog Won't Know

Marty Becker, D.V.M., and Gina Spadafori
with Illustrations by Molly Pearce

Health Communications, Inc.
Deerfield Beach, Florida

www.hcibooks.com

Library of Congress Cataloging-in-Publication Data

Becker, Marty, 1954-
    BowWow : curiously compelling facts, true tales & trivia even your
dog won't know / Marty Becker and Gina Spadafori ; illustrations by
Molly Pearce.
        p. cm.
    ISBN-13: 978-0-7573-0623-5 (trade paper)
    ISBN-10: 0-7573-0623-3 (trade paper)
    1. Dogs—Miscellanea. I. Spadafori, Gina. II. Title.
III. Title: Bow wow.
SF426.2.B44 2007
636.7—dc22

                                                                    2007032433

Publisher: Health Communications, Inc.
            3201 S.W. 15th Street
            Deerfield Beach, FL 33442-8190

Cover design by Larissa Hise Henoch
Interior design by Lawna Patterson Oldfield
Interior formatting by Dawn Von Strolley Grove

expressions—the smile. That means while you're smiling your way through this book, your dog will be enjoying it, too. So read on—you'll both be happier for the fun and the facts we fellow dog lovers have packed inside these covers.

Dr. Marty Becker
Gina Spadafori

Canine vitals

A DOG'S HEART NORMALLY beats between 70 to 180 times per minute, with little dogs having a faster heart rate. A puppy will also have a faster pulse—up to 220 beats per minute. You can take your dog's pulse at home, by the way, but not by putting your fingertips on your dog's wrist as you would with a person. Instead, check the heart rate in one of two places:

Choice 1: Put your hand over your dog's left side, behind the front leg. You'll feel the heart pulsing beneath your fingers. (If you can't, you might talk to your veterinarian about getting some of the fat off your dog.)

Choice 2: Put your fingertips on the femoral artery, located on the inside of the back leg just where it meets the body, and right in the middle. (It's a pretty big blood vessel, so you shouldn't have any problem finding it.)

Either way, count the beats while fifteen seconds clicks off your watch; multiply by four to get the BPM, or beats per minute. Do it when your dog is healthy and relaxed, so you'll know what's normal.

Normal canine body temperature is between 101.5 and 102 degrees, give or take a degree. You can use a traditional thermometer, or one of those newer ones that takes an electronic reading from the ear canal. (If you use the non-ear kind, be sure to take an indelible-ink marker and clearly write "dog" on the one you plan to use for your dog, so there's no confusion. You don't want something in your mouth that has been in your dog's fanny!)

Old Drums will never be forgotten

WHILE HUMANKIND AND DOGS have had a long and productive partner-ship, it wasn't until 1870 that the phrase "man's best friend" became part of dog lore. A dog named Old Drum had been shot to death, and in a courtroom speech worthy of a Hollywood clas-sic—we see Gregory Peck in the role—country lawyer George Graham Vest left not a dry eye in the house while talking about the true value of a dog.

It worked. Old Drum's owner won the case, and George Vest became so famous that he was later elected to the U.S. Senate.

"The one absolutely unselfish friend that a man can have in this selfish world, the one that never deserts him, the one that never proves ungrateful or treacherous, is his dog," said Vest in a Warrensburg, Missouri, court that day. No doubt he remembered those in the Senate later in his life.

Old Drum, by the way, has never been forgotten. In 1958, Warrensburg put up a statue to honor the memory of a good hunting hound who was one man's best friend to the end.

In later years, Vest's tribute became one of the standards on sympathy cards sent out by veterinarians after a client lost a beloved pet. Playwright Eugene O'Neill's lovely 1940 tribute to his Dalmatian Blemie in "The Last Will and Testament of Silverdene Emblem O'Neill" also became a favorite.

Save your dogs tags — they may be valuable

P EOPLE HAVE ALWAYS WANTED some way to get a roving dog home. And government authorities have always wanted a way to either put a property tax on a dog or, in later years, ensure that the animal was vaccinated against rabies. Dogs have been licensed for centuries, but the idea of a tag to signify that a dog was "street legal" seems to date to the late nineteenth century, when Cincinnati, Ohio, started issuing tags on an annual basis, and other cities and states soon followed suit.

Although wooden tags for soldiers were used

in the U.S. Civil War to help identify the injured and the dead, it wasn't until World War I that American soldiers got metal tags as standard issue. The resemblance between the tags of soldiers and of dogs—along with a good dollop of droll military humor—soon had the new tags called "dog tags," a term that sticks to this day. The way people love to collect things, it's probably no surprise to anyone that there's an International Society of Animal License Collectors, and no small amount of buying and selling of tags on the Internet. Unfortunately, modern tags will be of little interest to future collectors. While governments used to issue some tags that were creative and downright adorable—shaped like doghouses, acorns, police shields, and more—today's tags are the height of utilitarian design.

That's why the old tags are valuable, with tags of whimsical appearance, decent condition, and age going for hundreds of dollars.

These records were no dogs

A HANDFUL OF HIT RECORDS referenced dogs in the titles, perhaps most notably the Elvis Presley 1956 cover of the blues song "Hound Dog." But three years earlier, Patti Page's song "(How Much Is) That Doggie in the Window?" topped the charts for eight weeks.

And how about a band named after a dog? The popular '70s hit-makers Three Dog Night—who wished "joy to the fishes in the deep blue sea," but didn't say one word to the dogs—took their name from Australian Aboriginal lingo, judging how cold a night was by how many dogs it took to snuggle with to stay warm.

And it's a good strategy, by the way, since a

dog's normal body temperature is just enough higher than a person's to make him a natural heating pad or furry hot water bottle in a pinch. That may be why we put up with dog fur on the comforter as we share our own beds with our pets.

Don't bite the man who names you

A HANDFUL OF BREEDS was named for people. Louis Dobermann, a German tax collector in the mid-nineteenth century, developed the elegant and protective breed that bears his name to, in the words of Britain's Kennel Club, "protect him and . . . 'encourage' slow payers." In the U.K., the second "n" is retained in the name of the breed, but it's missing in the American name of the dog—as are part of the breed's ears, since ear cropping is common in the United States but illegal in England.

The Parson Russell Terrier—more commonly known as the Jack Russell—was named after the Rev. John Russell, a Victorian-era clergyman with a fondness for hunting terriers. The Cavalier King Charles Spaniel was named after King Charles II—although the breed was named centuries after his death because the dog was redeveloped by fanciers in England after World War II, separating it from the King Charles Spaniel, which is known in the United States as the English Toy Spaniel, a favorite dog of the

CAFÉ LATTE

British gentry for centuries. There's also the Gordon Setter, named after the Duke of Gordon.

Arguably, you can say that the Saint Bernard was named after a person, but really, the breed was probably named after the monastery where the dogs became famous for their heroic rescue efforts. (This is no longer practiced, by the way. The monastery now "borrows" Saint Bernards from nearby towns for tourist season, but doesn't keep any otherwise.)

Then there's the Dandie Dinmont Terrier, who isn't named for a real person at all, but rather after a character in Sir Walter Scott's *Guy Mannering.* There's something else fairly unique about the long-bodied, short-legged dog with a puff of fur on his head and whiskers on his muzzle: Dandies are so rare that the breed is considered on the verge of extinction. Every year, more pandas are born than Dandies.

Side by side, they fight

DOGS HAVE ALWAYS GONE to war, serving as everything from spike-collared attack forces to munitions haulers, from messengers to modern-day sentries and bomb- and drug-sniffers. The dogs really stepped up in World War I, when more than fifteen thousand of them served as guard dogs, messengers, sentries, and rat-killers for Allied forces.

On the other side of the conflict, a young soldier with a handlebar mustache named Adolf Hitler took a real fancy to an English terrier who somehow managed to make it across No Man's Land and tumble into the future Führer's trench. Terriers were considered a real asset on the frontlines, dispatching vermin and providing an early-warning system for mortar and gas attacks. As lively as terriers are, they no doubt also relieved some of the stress of a soldier's life.

Hitler named his dog Fuchsl, or Little Fox, and was said to adore the animal, who was likely stolen from him in 1917.

The history of dogs in war is no prettier than that of war in general, and casualties are common. Militaries have often abandoned their dogs to the fates when bringing soldiers back home.

Many a soldier has owed his life to a dog, and many have never forgotten that debt. Organizations of former military dog handlers remain active, and among their goals are memorials to the animals who served so bravely.

Just say "Ahhhhhhh"

A LL DOGS HAVE PINK tongues, with two notable exceptions: the Chow Chow and the Chinese Shar-Pei, both breeds with tongues variously described as "purple," "black," or "blue-black." Both breeds originated in China, and Shar-Pei (the name refers to Chinese for "shark skin") was described in the 1970s as the rarest breed in the world.

Not so anymore. The dog best known for his wrinkles—and attendant skin problems, from a veterinary point of view—was forty-seventh out of more than 150 breeds registered by the American Kennel Club in 2006.

Black spots on tongues are common in many

dogs, and are not necessarily an indication that there's a Chow Chow or Shar-Pei in the gene pool.

How do dogs measure up?

WHILE WE HUMANS measure our height to the top of our heads, the height of a dog is measured at the highest point of the shoulder, called the withers. The tallest living dog is a California Great Dane named Gibson, who is 42.4 inches at the withers, but more than seven feet tall when standing on two legs.

In general, though, the Irish Wolfhound is considered the tallest breed of dog.

The recent trend toward ultra-tiny dogs has a lot of petite pups being carried around, but the smallest so far is a Chihuahua named Heaven Sent Brady, who measured six inches from nose to tail tip.

The heaviest breed of dog is the English Mastiff. For the biggest of the big, you have to go back a few years. Zorba de la-Susa, a male English Mastiff born in London, was certified as the world's heaviest dog at 343 pounds. Zorba, who was born in 1981 and died in November 1989, was also the world's longest dog at eight feet three inches long.

And that brings up an important point: while we love superlatives—biggest, smallest, and so on—when it comes to our dogs, breeds that are extreme in any way tend to struggle with chronic illness and die young. It doesn't really seem fair that these animals should suffer because of human whims when it comes to how dogs should look.

Nature seems to have limits to just how far we can push the design of dogs, and we go beyond those lines at peril to our pets.

No White House can be home without a dog

PRESIDENT HARRY S. TRUMAN once said, "If you want a friend in Washington, get a dog." There's no doubt U.S. presidents have always gravitated toward the canine set, probably both for reasons of companionship and politics. (The latter because Americans have always seemed to appreciate the man who can appreciate a good dog.)

The father of the country set the tone for this canine adoration: President George Washington was known for his love of foxhounds, and the genes of his prized pack are probably in some of these hounds even today.

Among modern-day First Dogs, perhaps none

is more famous than Fala, the Scottish Terrier who saw President Franklin Delano Roosevelt through the trying years of World War II. Fala's devotion is memorialized in stone at the FDR monument in Washington, D.C., where a likeness of the little terrier sits forever at his master's side. (FDR also had six other dogs, but who ever heard of them? Fala reigns supreme!)

Although President George W. Bush is also a fan of the Scottish terrier, with Barney and Miss Beazley starring in their own videos, his father President George Herbert Walker Bush had another of the most well-known of presidential pooches—the Springer Spaniel Millie, who "wrote" a best-selling book and promoted literacy during her term of office.

Having a dog isn't always such a good thing, though. After Lucky the Bouvier resisted attempts at house-training and embarrassed the

First Lady by dragging her across the White House lawn, President Ronald W. Reagan banished the big bouncy beastie to their California ranch. Nancy Reagan then picked out a more promising pup, a diminutive and well-mannered Cavalier King Charles Spaniel named Rex.

And President Lyndon Baines Johnson caused a national furor when he picked up one of his beagles up by the ears. Pet lovers put the president in the proverbial doghouse, despite his protestations that Him and Her liked such treatment—along with, one assumes, their unimaginative names.

The other thing Helen Keller is famous for

HELEN KELLER, the blind and deaf Alabama girl whose triumph over her disabilities made her an international sensation, was the first American to own an Akita.

On a speaking tour of Japan in the days before World War II, Keller became infatuated with the courage, loyalty, and lore of the Japanese breed, and was promised a dog of her own. A breeder offered her an adult, but then realized a puppy was better suited. The puppy was Kamikaze-Go, called Kami by Keller.

Before preventive vaccines became standard veterinary practice, distemper outbreaks used to claim many dogs. Unfortunately, one of them was Kami, who died at seven months of age. On hearing of her grief, the breeder sent another dog, a littermate to Kami—Kenzan-Go, called Go-Go by Keller.

Give me casting . . . there needs to be a change

LASSIE STARTED OUT as a collie in the short story that inspired her (um, his—the real Lassie was a boy playing a girl) career. But at least one other dog changed his breed from page to screen. As written by Dashiell Hammett, Asta the dog in *The Thin Man* was a Miniature Schnauzer, but on the silver screen the role was performed by a Wire Fox Terrier.

It's not a casting change on par with imagining Ronald Reagan staring in *Casablanca* instead of Humphrey Bogart, though, since both breeds are small, fuzzy-faced, and very stylish, with an air of obvious superiority.

Names of yesteryear

DOGS TODAY are more likely to be given human names: Sam, Sadie, Molly, Max. But it wasn't always so. At least two names — Rover and Fido — were once so popular that they now serve as synonyms for the word "dog."

These names were of the descriptive variety, revealing the traits a dog had — or those his owners hoped he'd have. Rover is pretty obvious, a term from the days before leash laws became more common than not. But Fido? Its roots are Latin and suggest a dog of unflinching loyalty and courage (rather like the motto of the U.S. Marine Corps, Semper Fi, or always faithful).

Today, when you meet a dog named Fido, it's likely the owner gave the name as a sort of kitschy joke, even more so if the name is dressed up as "Fideaux" or some other such silliness.

English, American . . . it's still a Cocker Spaniel, sort of

THE BRITS DEVELOPED the Cocker Spaniel, a hardy, happy little hunting dog whose specialty was helping with the finding and fetching of woodcock, which is where the name came from. But American show breeders developed a dog that looked different enough that the breed soon became split into two types: American and English.

In the United States, the "Cocker Spaniel" is the American type, a dog with so much coat on the underside that those winning in the show ring look as if they're wearing a floor-length skirt. These "furnishings" are such dirt magnets that the feet of show cockers hit the actual ground as little as possible during their careers. The American cocker also has a shorter, broader, and more rounded head.

In the United Kingdom, the "Cocker Spaniel" is the English type, with less fur and a longer, leaner head, and a more racy appearance overall.

Not surprisingly, names are the game on both sides of the pond. In the United States, the

American-style dog is called the Cocker Spaniel, while the English-style is called the English Cocker Spaniel. In the U.K. it's the reverse: The home of the Cocker recognizes only its own variety as authentic, and calls the colonial version the American Cocker Spaniel.

No matter the variety, the Cocker Spaniel has been a reliable family companion for generations, although the breed's popularity has waned since the heady days when a Cocker named My Own Brucie became a coast-to-coast sensation for being named Best in Show at the prestigious Westminster Kennel Club twice, and *Lady and the Tramp* was box-office magic for Disney. (Lady herself was drawn more as an English Cocker than an American one.)

Don't enter

THE PHRASE "BEWARE OF DOG" is so old that its Latin equivalent—*cave canem*—has been found on signs in Roman ruins. The word "watchdog" isn't quite as old; the first mention of it: by Shakespeare, in *The Tempest*.

Brachis . . . brecha . . . brukuh . . . oh, heck, just say "pug-nosed"

DOGS WITH EXTREMELY short muzzles and rounded heads are called brachycephalic, and despite their adorable, almost human expressions, they have a host of related health challenges related to the non-standard-issue canine anatomy. Quite a few breeds large and small fit into this category, from the popular Pug (which as "Pug-nosed" gives a friendlier term to all such dogs) to Bulldogs and Boxers. ("Brachycephalic" comes from Greek roots, combining words for "short" and "head" to define these dogs perfectly.)

Perhaps most notable to their human owners is their tendency to snore and be gassy. Some of them are also droolers because their faces don't fit together as well as those of other dogs.

From the dog's point of view, being pug-nosed isn't much of a plus. The dogs are notoriously heat-intolerant, and they have such difficulty breathing that air travel is generally not recommended. The malformation of the skull often results in crowding of teeth that can cause dental issues.

And then there's the matter of their eyes: because there isn't a lot of room for eye sockets, the relatively large, round eyes that give these breeds their endearing appearance have a tendency to pop out in response to rough play or other head trauma. And the folds of skin can be difficult to maintain, with infections being common.

Veterinarians can correct some of these issues with surgery that may seem cosmetic but can actually improve quality of life for these pets.

The name "pug," by the way, may be derived from the Latin word *pugnis,* meaning fist, presumably because the silhouette of the dog's head resembles one. Some pug owners affectionately call their dogs Puglies (combo of Pug and ugly).

An unwilling passenger

LAIKA, A STRAY RUSSIAN pup who was likely part husky, was the first earthly being sent into space, in 1957 on *Sputnik 2*, triggering a space race between the United States and Russia at the height of the Cold War.

Since Laika was a sacrificial lamb—or dog, to be precise—with no provisions made for her return, it's probably just as well she apparently died not long after takeoff. "Laika," by the way, is Russian for "bark."

Who forgot the space heaters

EVERYWHERE PEOPLE have traveled, dogs have gone with them — even to the ends of the Earth. In the early days of polar exploration, explorers relied on dog sleds, using teams of working dogs to pull people and supplies across an unforgiving wilderness.

But at least one dog on Admiral Richard Byrd's famous explorations of Antarctica wasn't along to pull a sled. Byrd's dog was Igloo, a Fox Terrier who was equipped with fur-lined boots and a camel-hair coat. Sounds stylish!

Dogs play poker
while art critics wince

WHILE CLASSIC DOG art merits its own New York gallery, and art depicting the prized dogs of the rich commands sky-high prices at auction, it's no chump bet that the most famous painting with dogs in it is delightfully low-class, and proud of it.

Commonly known as the "Dogs Playing Poker" pictures, these gems date to 1903, when Cassius Marcellus Coolidge produced them for a Minnesota advertising agency. While they may not have attracted much notice then or had much value, the ensuing years have been kind to the pieces.

Two of them—"A Bold Bluff" and "Waterloo"— were auctioned off in 2005, fetching more the $600,000 for the pair.

If you ever find yourself with a team of sled dogs . . .

D ESPITE THE POPULAR misconception, sled dogs do not start running when the driver yells "mush." "Hike" is the sled-dog equivalent of punching the gas pedal. Other commands the dogs are trained to respond to include "haw" (left), "gee" (right), "on by" (for passing), and the ever popular "whoa" (Stop! Please stop!).

Top competitors train nearly year-round. When the snow disappears, they use a sled with wheels to keep their dogs fit. Competitive sled dogs, by the way, aren't usually purebreds, but rather a dog called the Alaskan husky, bred for work and speed by mixing in many other breeds.

A dog named Indiana

INDIANA JONES, THE adventuring arche-ologist played by Harrison Ford in a string of hit movies, took his name from a dog. Moviemaker George Lucas had a dog named Indiana as a child and worked with Stephen Spielberg on the *Indiana Jones* movies.

It's not the only time Indiana influenced a bit of Hollywood history. Lucas has said the Wookiee species—and Chewbacca in particu-lar—is based on Indiana, who was a Malamute.

Giving blood
for a good cause

EVERY DAY, SICK or injured dogs require blood transfusions as part of their treatment. That blood comes from canine blood donors.

The use of blood products for treating sick and injured pets has increased so dramatically that there is a growing shortage of canine and feline blood. Several commercial blood banks have opened in response to this need, and many veterinary practices have developed their own blood banks.

The donated blood is used in the same way that blood is used in human medical facilities: as whole blood, plasma, and packed red cells. The blood is collected in sterile plastic bags, and is handled and stored in the same way as human blood.

Although most stored blood comes from "professional" donors—typically dogs living in a veterinary hospital or, more recently, retired racing greyhounds kept in colonies as blood donors—in some areas, canine blood drives are held. The blood is donated—you can't earn money from your dog's donation—but it's certainly for a worthy cause.

By the way, most dogs kept as blood donors are adopted out after a relatively short period of service. Since they're chosen for their size (bigger dog equals more blood) and temperament (must be easygoing), these dogs make wonderful pets.

Good reasons
for a snip-snip

UNSPAYED FEMALES usually come into season for a few weeks twice a year, during which you need to deal with a varying amount of mess and the constant attention of canine suitors. Unneutered males may be less than attentive when such attractions beckon and may migrate to the next ZIP Code in search of love. They can also be more likely to challenge your leadership—or anyone else's.

Studies have shown, for example, that young, unneutered males are most likely to be involved in attacks on children. Spaying or neutering generally makes dogs of both genders easier to live with, but especially for males by decreasing undesirable behaviors, such as fighting, territorialism, and urine-marking.

But there are health advantages, too. Altering a pet prevents reproductive cancers, as well as a potentially deadly reproductive infection called pyometra unspayed females.

The common flea?
It's the cat flea

THE FLEAS FOUND on dogs are usually "cat fleas." In fact, although there are hundreds of species of fleas around the world, the cat

flea causes most of the irritation in the United States.

Blaming cats for fleas isn't fair, though. The cat flea got the name because the person who first identified the parasite did so after pulling one from a cat. He could have just as easily pulled one from a dog and given dogs the blame.

Or maybe because dogs generally suffer more from fleas than cats do, cats are happy to take credit.

Have you shot your dog yet?

MORE PEOPLE SEE to it that their pets are properly vaccinated against disease than their children. Some three-quarters of pre-school children have received all their immunizations, but when you look at pets, the compliance rate is 10 percent higher.

That said, a lot of dog lovers aren't aware that "yearly" shots are no longer routinely given for adult dogs. Depending on a risk assessment of each individual pet (based on breed, age, life stage, lifestyle, etc.), some vaccines, such as those for kennel cough or a new dental vaccine, may be given every year, while vaccinations for distemper and parvovirus may be given every three years. In recent years, veterinary schools and colleges have been recommending that many boosters be given at three-year intervals. One major exception is rabies, which is governed as much by public-health pressures as veterinary ones. While many states and municipalities have gone to a three-year rabies shot, others still require annual boosters.

Even without yearly shots, your dog should still be seeing your veterinarian at least annually for a thorough checkup. Dogs by their nature try to hide illnesses, can't tell us where it hurts, and age much faster than humans. Diseases caught early are always easier and usually cheaper to treat.

Salute the all-Americans

WHILE MANY BREEDS of dogs were developed in the United Kingdom, more than a few breeds are "Made in America." Perhaps the most surprising of the lot is the Australian shepherd, which isn't Australian at all.

Other breeds developed in the United States include the American Dingo (Carolina Dog), Alaskan Malamute, American Eskimo Dog, American Foxhound, American Water Spaniel, American Staffordshire Terrier, Boykin Spaniel, Catahoula Leopard Dog, various Coonhounds (including Black and Tan and Bluetick), Boston Terrier, Chesapeake Bay Retriever, and the Toy Fox Terrier.

The Canadians have a few native breeds, too, including the Nova Scotia Duck Tolling Retriever, the Labrador Retriever and the Newfoundland.

Hair club for dogs

WHILE MOST DOGS have fur that will grow to a genetically determined length and then stop, the coats of some dogs will keep growing and growing.

The Komondor, a large herd-protecting breed that resembles nothing so much as a large mop on the move, has fur that develops into cords—think dreadlocks—that will get so long they sweep the ground. (The same is true of the Puli.) The fur is said to protect these herd dogs from nasty winter weather. The Bergamasco, an Italian flock-protecting breed, employs a similar strategy, except that in this breed, the coat forms not long, roapy cords but something that can be more accurately described as big chunks of felt-like mats.

Although very few people choose to keep their poodles in such fashion—coat maintenance is a lot of work—the fur of these dogs will also form into cords if allowed to continue growing. Instead, poodle breeders craft their dogs like topiary, with areas of well-groomed fluff on the

front of the animal and closely shaved skin elsewhere. (The use of hair extensions on the areas that are supposed to be long, though not strictly allowed, is nonetheless not uncommon in top show dogs.)

Dogs with coats that require a lot of work during a show career are typically sheared of their gorgeous locks when they revert to privileged pets and parents.

Teeth, by the numbers

DOGS ARE AMAZINGLY well adapted to their original purpose—a versatile eater of almost anything—through the virtue of their teeth.

They have forty-two of them (puppies have twenty-eight), but that's not the whole story. Adult dogs have four different kinds of teeth—incisors, canines, premolars, and molars. Although the collection isn't well-suited to grinding down material, the teeth are good for getting meals fresh—as in, on your own—or dealing with whatever you may find in a day of doggie travel. (The puppy collection is missing molars because they don't have to grind food as they're tugging on Mom's teats and are on a liquid diet.)

Those large and significant canines attract the most attention, and in fact the teeth are so famous that even in other species—cats and

humans, for example—those "fangs" are called "canines."

Puppies start losing their baby teeth at around four months of age. The incisors fall first, then the canines at about six months, and finally the molars. The adult teeth push the baby teeth out, and all that puppy chewing helps the process, while also making a puppy feel better about the discomfort associated with teething. Now and then, though, a baby tooth will be retained, a situation quickly remedied by the veterinarian with a quick yank during a puppy visit.

Canine geography lessons

THE GREAT DANE isn't Danish at all, but rather traces back to Germany. And the Dalmatian appears to have very little reason to be named for Dalmatia, a region in the Balkans.

Other breed names accurately reflect their country of origin, including the Chihuahua (from a state in Mexico), many of the terriers (notably the Scottish and West Highland, but also the Border Terrier, named for the region between England and Scotland), the Belgian herding breeds (Tervuren, Malinois, Groendal and Lackinois—the same dog, just different coats) and the Rottweiler, which is named for a town in Germany.

And how about the Briard, which shares the origin of its name with a cheese? Both hail from Brie, the famed cheese-making region.

Dogs win, biblically speaking

DOGS ARE MENTIONED a few dozen times in the Bible. Cats are not mentioned at all. Only one breed of dog is mentioned by name in The Good Book: The Greyhound.

Hollywood's first Big Dog

RIN TIN TIN was voted the most popular film entertainer in 1926. Imagine a silent movie star with a bite but no bark. The German Shepherd always kept it real, however, perhaps remembering his hard times as a puppy in a bombed-out French dog kennel before he was saved by a U.S. soldier in World War I. The dog was named after a popular French puppet given to soldiers for luck.

Rin Tin Tin made more than two dozen films and was just shy of his fifteenth birthday when he died in the arms of Jean Harlow. Not a bad life for a war orphan with doggy breath!

Star-gazing with dogs

THE "DOG DAYS" of summer—late July and early August—derive their name from the star Sirius, named for Orion's two-headed hound from Greek mythology. During the "dog days," Sirius is at its most visible. Dog days, then, have nothing to do with heat and everything to do with what's going on overhead. The term, by the way, traces back to ancient Rome.

Clicking with your dog

WHILE IT'S NO SECRET that a lot of
dogs can't "hold their licker," professional photographers have long had a secret for
getting those endearing images of dogs and puppies kissing on kids.

Butter.

That's right, rub a little butter on the cheek of
the child and there's not a dog in the world that
won't "help" by cleaning the kid's face.

And while we're talking about great dog
shots, here are some more tips. First, go out-
side. Although new cameras and software have
made it easier to remove the dreaded red-eye
from images, dogs generally look better in

natural light. Look beyond your dog and make sure your background is clean and complementary. You don't want a pole appearing to stick out of your dog's back, nor do you want your precious pup to be lost in a cluttered background.

A helper is always handy. You can set up your dog any way you want, tell him to "stay," and then have your helper get his attention with treats or a squeaky toy. If your dog's reliable on "stay," throw the toy—the motion will get the dog's attention every time.

Snap!

How now, brown dog?

WHAT'S WRONG with the color brown? Nothing . . . except that people who draw up the "blueprints" for dog breeds don't seem to like it much. Like interior designers and the people who dream up names for paint colors, it seems the kennel-club set thinks "brown" is just too boring a word.

Instead, purebred dogs tend to come in "sable," "beige," "fawn," "mahogany," "Isabella" (which is further described as fawn), and "tan." Not many breeds list plain ol' brown among their acceptable colors.

Still, if you're going for something to make you drool over a good-looking dog, wouldn't you rather have a "chocolate" Labrador than a "liver" Springer Spaniel?

Clearly, the Labrador people have a more creative marketing department.

And when they catch you, they'll lick you

BLOODHOUNDS AREN'T so named because they're bloodthirsty, or because they follow a trail of blood. They're named because they were originally the dogs of the aristocracy—the folks we might today call "blue bloods."

Despite the images of Bloodhounds chasing criminals through the swamps, for the Bloodhound it's all about the chase and nothing personal. Unlike dogs trained for police work, who seem all too happy to "take a bite out of crime," the Bloodhound would rather give the object of his quest a slurp than a snarl at the end of it.

The Bloodhound's ability to differentiate

scents is so good that his work is acceptable as evidence in a court of law. One of the physical attributes—besides a big nose—that helps with the work are the folds of skin and long, floppy ears, which help to hold scent near the dog's nose.

Although using hounds to track criminals no doubt goes back much farther, history marks 1805 as the date when the Thrapthon Association for the Prevention of Felons got a Bloodhound to help in their work.

All you need to nose

WHY DO DOGS have cold noses? One story attributes it to Noah's Ark, saying that the dog was the last one aboard and so got stuck with his nose exposed for forty days and forty nights. When the floodwaters went away, the story goes, the nose was permanently chilled.

The truth isn't so fanciful. A dog's nose is cooled because it's designed to stay wet, and evaporation keeps it cool.

Tears are constantly produced to lubricate the movement of the eyes. Because this lubrication is so critical to eye health, the dog's body routine produces more tears than are needed. These excess tears flow through the naso-lacrimal (literally "nose-tears") duct and out the base of the nose. (People experience this when crying.)

As the tears drip down into the dog's face, the dog licks her nose, spreading the tear fluid over the nose, which wets it. Then, evaporation causes the nose to be cool. The moistened nose is better equipped to dissolve airborne chemicals, which contributes to a better sense of smell.

So what about the idea that a dog is sick when her nose is warm and dry? There's a little truth to it. When a dog is sick, the body uses up more internal water in the process of fighting disease. This increased use, especially with a fever, causes relative dehydration, even if the dog is drinking a normal amount of water. This dehydration results in deceased tear production, and hence a dry nose.

Sniff sniff sniff . . .
I smell a CD

IS THERE ANYTHING a dog can't use his nose to figure out? Dogs have long been used to sniff out escaped cons and missing children (think Bloodhounds), dinner (think Pointers), and even truffles (think Poodles). But in recent years trainers have come up with all kinds of new ways to use the dog's extraordinary sense of smell. Here are a few you maybe knew—and a few more we bet you did not.

Drugs: Dogs can be trained to sniff out all kinds of illegal drugs, finding them not only on people, but also in massive cargo containers, long-haul trucks, and school lockers.

Plant matters: Since fresh fruit and vegetables

can bring in insects and diseases with the potential to cause great damage to agriculture, dogs are used to detect the foodstuffs in the luggage of people coming through customs. Dogs are also used to sniff out invasive weeds in the field, so the plants can be eradicated before they take hold.

Insects: Termites? No problem. Dogs are also being used to detect the resurgence of bed bugs in big cities.

Mold: Dogs sniff out not only the mold that bedevils homeowners, but also mold that puts the vines at wineries at risk from the spread of disease.

Explosives: Meetings of high public officials would be hard to imagine without the diligent work of bomb-sniffing dogs. To take it a bit further, dogs are even being taught to sniff out cell phones that could be used to detonate a bomb.

Cows in heat: A lot of money depends on being able to artificially inseminate a cow without wasting time guessing when she's ready. While a bull could tell, he's not usually available, as his contribution usually arrives frozen on the scene. A dog can tell when the cow is most fertile—although it's a good bet he couldn't care less.

Cancer: While cancer detection is still in the trial stage, it's looking pretty promising that dogs can spot a malignancy. Some day your doctor may order up a "Lab test" and mean Labrador!

Chemicals: Dogs have been taught to look for items as varied as mercury and the components of potentially pirated DVDs.

While most of us tend to think scent work is the near-exclusive province of a handful of breeds—Bloodhounds, German Shepherds and maybe the odd Labrador—in fact a wide range

of breeds and mixes can be trained to detect various scents. Because of their fine noses and friendly dispositions, Beagles are used to work airports by the U.S. Department of Agriculture, and any number of mixed breeds—lucky dogs pulled from shelters—has been used for other kinds of detection work.

Because all dogs have keen noses filled with dozens more scent receptors than we humans have, a dog's future doing nose work relies more on enthusiasm, reliability, and trainability than on the canine-common ability to tell one scent from another.

When a dog show was all about the Sensation

THE DOG SHOW was an invention of Victorian England. Before people got the idea to breed animals to look a certain way, dogs were purposely bred for their usefulness, which meant ability was more important than looks. Other dogs were left to their own scavenging ways, breeding when they could—with the result pretty much looking like the modern-day dingo. (These so-called pariah-type dogs still exist in many of the nonindustrialized countries.)

Human nature being what it is, though, the people of the moneyed, leisure classes of England soon decided to start competing against one another to decide which of their dogs were

the best-looking. Americans weren't far behind in setting up such competitions.

In the United States, the first dog show came about after a bunch of rich guys started bragging about their dogs while socializing at the Westminster Hotel in Manhattan. The hotel's long gone, but the name lives on in the world-famous Westminster Kennel Club dog show, held in New York City since 1877. Westminster is still the top show on the American dog-show scene, and as a sporting event, its longevity is second only to the Kentucky Derby.

The Westminster Kennel Club's logo is of a pointer named Sensation, who in his home country of England was known by the somewhat less exciting moniker of Don. We're guessing the rich sportsman who imported him wanted him to sound well worth the big dough he no doubt shelled out for the dog.

Westminster predated the formation of the American Kennel Club by several years and was also the first American dog show to choose an overall Best in Show, for which mockumentary filmmaker Christopher Guest is surely grateful.

Insurance agents don't much like these dogs

A S PEOPLE HAVE become ever-more-willing to sue over dog bites—perhaps because almost every city now has a personal-injury lawyer who chases not ambulances but animal-control trucks—some insurers have decided to deny homeowners insurance to people whose pets are certain breeds.

These breeds often include Pit Bull terriers, Akitas, Chow Chows, Dobermans, German Shepherds, Rottweilers and the Presa Canario, a breed that many heard of for the first time after a pair of them killed a woman in the landing of a San Francisco apartment building.

As might be expected, people who love these

dogs argue it's not fair to assume they are all dangerous. In many states, the legislatures have considered passing laws to prohibit breed discrimination—as well as all-out breed bans.

Breed bans aren't uncommon, though, with Denver perhaps the biggest city to prohibit Pit Bulls from within its borders.

Strong dog, indeed

O<small>N</small> A<small>UGUST</small> 11, 1974, the Saint Bernard Kashwitna set a world record by pulling six thousand pounds on wheels and won the title of World's Strongest Dog in the *Guinness Book of World Records.* His brother Susitna later set the world record, still unchallenged, for a weight pull on snow, by pulling 5,220 pounds at the 1976 World Championship Dog Weight Pull.

Talk about a trouper!

THE SHOW MUST GO ON, and Sandy sure knew it. The star of the long-running

Broadway hit *Annie!* saw a lot of tomorrows, playing the entire run from 1977 to 1983—more than two thousand performances. The friendly fuzzbutt—probably an Airedale-setter mix—came from a shelter in Connecticut.

After all those curtain calls, the dog retired to the comfortable life befitting such a star and died in 1990 at the grand old age of sixteen.

Lick, lick, and heel . . . er . . . heal

THE IDEA THAT A DOG'S saliva has healing powers has been around at least since the ancient Greeks and Romans, whose physicians believed it to be an antidote for poisoning. Later, Saint Roch was often pictured with a dog licking a sore, reflecting the belief that the patron saint of plague victims knew something about a cure and that his dog's saliva had made him healthy.

Modern medicine doesn't look kindly on such theories, especially when the things a dog eats and licks are taken into account. So if you have a cut, try a little antiseptic spray and a bandage instead.

Sure, this is a little gross, but you're dying to know: Dogs like to lick wounds because the serum that leaks from an open sore is sweet.

Modern breeds,
ancient histories

MOST BREEDS ARE relatively new to the scene, developed within the last century or two to fill a specific niche by people—think rich—who had a lot of time on their hands to develop a breed and "set type," or develop a standard to be followed for generations and have dogs that breed largely "true" to that standard.

Before the great age of breed creations, there were a few generally established types of dogs, such as the Greyhound and other who hunted by running game down, the large and imposing breeds of the Mastiff family, and the small, tough vermin-killers that served as the pest-control services of their day.

One breed that seems ancient really isn't at all. The Pharaoh Hound, once thought to date back to ancient Egypt, has been more recently revealed through DNA analysis to be a re-creation of the ancient hound, probably through the breeding of a couple of European hunting dogs and then further refined for the right "look."

Perhaps this little historical sleight of hand is why the Pharaoh Hound is the only breed of dog to blush. When excited, their ears become pink-ish. (Maybe their cheeks turn pink, too, but with the fur on them, who can tell?)

The oldest dog ever?

AUSTRALIAN CATTLE DOGS and Queensland Heelers are known for being generally healthy, tough, and long-lived dogs, but one of them is also a record-holder along those lines. Bluey was a genuinely *Australian* Australian Cattle Dog—he lived in Victoria—and he is thought have set the mark for being the oldest dog ever, living to the incredible age of twenty-nine before his death in 1939.

Lassie wasn't the first collie to make a splash

BEFORE LASSIE EVER CAME HOME, a queen and a top-selling author had already taken the breed from a humble shepherd's workmate to a high-fashion celebrity must-have.

The collie—the name is thought to have been derived from a black-and-white breed of sheep—was elevated to high society by England's Queen Victoria, who adored the dogs and considered them the perfect royal companion. She was followed in her admiration by Albert Payson Terhune, whose best-selling *Lad: A Dog* was the first of a string of books and short stories that made him one of the best-selling writers in the years between the World Wars.

The world was ready for a collie star when Eric Knight's 1938 short story about his boyhood dog made a splash in *The Saturday Evening Post.* "Lassie Come Home" was soon a movie, and the beautiful collie—a boy dog playing a girl, because of the showier coat—was soon a major star.

For baby boomers, though, the Lassie best remembered is likely the TV version, which debuted in 1954 and has long been parodied for seemingly telepathic communication between the dog and his owners. ("What is it, Lassie? Timmy fell into the well? Show me!")

Today's Lassie—still in the care of the Weatherwax family—is a direct descendant of the first of the famous movie collies, and still works as an actor and advertising pitch dog, with great success.

Collies, by the way, come in many more varieties than the "Lassie look," which is officially

known as sable. There's also a short-haired variety called the Smooth Collie, which is exactly the
same except for coat length. And both varieties
come in more colors than the one made recogniz-
able by Lassie, including blue merle (a mix of
gray and black hairs) and tri-color (a black sad-
dle over white bib, with tan markings). Collies
even come in white, which was the color of
President Calvin Coolidge's pair, Rob Roy and
Prudence Prim.

Art for the dog-minded

SIR EDWIN LANDSEER (1802–1873) is perhaps the best—and certainly the best known—painter who made his living painting the animals of the privileged. Landseer's ability to capture the grace and beauty of his patrons' dogs made him so famous and successful that a variety of Newfoundland—the black-and-white Landseer—bears his name.

Landseer works fetch top dollars at art auctions, and they are highly sought after by art collectors and dog lovers alike.

Another interesting tidbit about Sir Edwin: the popular image of a Saint Bernard with a cask hanging from the collar comes not from real life, but from a Landseer painting. This image became so ingrained into the culture that some people started adorning their dogs with casks for special occasions.

A smashing way
to sell biscuits

CRUFTS, HELD ANNUALLY in Birmingham, England, is the world's largest dog show, routinely drawing more than twenty thousand dogs into the halls of the massive National Exhibition Centre over its four-day run. The show debuted in London in 1891 when Charles Cruft, a traveling dog-biscuit salesman, thought it up. Even the queen thought it was a wonderful idea, entering some of her dogs. The show has been a smash ever since.

Because of the strict rabies laws of the United Kingdom—which is, and wishes to remain, free of the disease—the show was largely for the natives because few foreign dog-show fanciers wanted to kennel their dogs for the six-month quarantine. The easing of the laws in recent years has seen more foreign dogs in competition. In 2006, an American Australian Shepherd with an American professional handler won Best in Show, earning the stiff-upper-lip disapproval of all the traditionalists in attendance, no doubt.

Panting to stay cool

COMPARED TO THEIR owners, dogs have very few sweat glands. There are some in the paw pads, so dogs do sweat from their feet, as well as from other relatively less furry regions of their bodies. But the primary way dogs cool off is by panting.

Panting is very rapid, shallow breathing that enhances the evaporation of water from the tongue, mouth, and upper respiratory tract. Evaporation dissipates heat as water vapor.

Panting can reach frequencies of 300 to 400 breaths per minute. (The normal canine breathing rate is thirty to forty breaths per minute.) Yet it requires surprisingly little effort. Because of the natural elasticity of the lungs and airways, panting does not expend much energy nor create additional heat.

And that's a good thing because dogs are very easily overheated and prone to heat stroke in hot weather, especially when the humidity is also high (which minimizes the effectiveness of panting).

Why male dogs have one more bone than females

WHEN A MALE DOG becomes sexually aroused, there really is a rock-hard bone—called the *os penis*—at the core of approximately half the penis. The bone is also present in a flaccid penis. You can't see the *os penis*, of course (except on an x-ray), but you can't see a dog's nonerect penis either; it remains completely hidden inside the prepuce, which is a protective sheath of skin, kind of like a sausage casing.

Are you my dad?
Are you? Are you?

Puppies in the same litter can have different fathers, depending on how many dogs Mom had access to while in season. While sometimes

this multiple-dad development happens by accident, that's not always the case.

Sometimes a breeder will give her dog access to two sires in real life or artificially inseminate either with fresh, overnighted semen or by frozen "dadsicles." (The latter method gives a breeder access to a great stud dog who has passed on, but left a little something of himself behind in a canine sperm bank.) When the puppies are born, DNA testing sorts out the parentage issues for the purpose of pedigrees.

The same DNA technology has also been used in a handful of "pupernity" suits to get the owner of a free-roaming Romeo to pay a share of the expenses.

Dig this! And this! And this!

TO THE CHAGRIN of any dog lover who also wants a lush backyard, digging is both a natural and manmade behavior.

Nordic breeds—such as Malamutes and Huskies—tend to be diggers because their commonalities with the wolf run a little deeper than among other breeds. For them, the desire to dig is natural, and it can be quite strong. In the snow, they know to dig themselves a nice little cave to stay warm if they're caught out in the elements. In the heat, they know to dig down into the ground to stay just a little bit cooler.

In Terriers, though, digging is a natural dog drive ramped up by generations of selective breeding. Terriers—the very name comes from *terra,* Latin for "earth"—were developed to "go to ground" after everything from mice and rats to badgers, foxes, and groundhogs. These fearless little dogs will dig after any prey—or just dig, if there's nothing better to do.

Help wanted: dog-style

TRADITIONAL JOBS FOR DOGS include protecting people and property, herding, hunting, and pulling sleds or carts. Modern dogs who are trained for these activities are often competing in sports, not working for a living. These sports simulate the jobs dogs once worked at for their keep, and they are thought to help keep breeds true to the work for which they were developed (so we never end up with, say, Labrador retrievers who are interested neither in swimming nor retrieving).

Today, though, a dog is more likely to find work in show business than helping the milkman deliver dairy products to homes. (Note to anyone younger than fifty: milkmen used to deliver dairy products to homes. You'll just have to trust us on this one, although neither author is old enough to remember when this was done with a dog- or horse-drawn cart.)

While many of the old-time jobs have been largely phased out, there's plenty of new work for dogs. Many jobs involve sniffing out things (as mentioned elsewhere in this book), but others involve being helpful to people who need a little help. Service dogs fill a wide range of needs and include dogs who help people with impaired vision or hearing, or those who use wheelchairs.

There's a dog sport born every minute (almost)

WHEN ALEX STEIN and his dog, Ashley Whippet, eluded security at a nationally televised baseball game in 1974 to show off the dog's skill at catching flying discs, little did Stein know a new dog sport was about to be born. Up until that time, most competitive canine endeavors were based on such traditional dog skills as hunting or herding, but that was about to change.

Ashley Whippet was soon getting a national audience for acrobatics, and other dog lovers were jumping into newly formed competitions with their own high-flying canines. (Flying disc competitions also proved to be a boon for veterinary surgeons because all the leaping, twisting, and landing proved to be more than a little hard on canine knees and other joints.)

Since then, new dog sports have been invented and developed devoted followings. The most popular among them is canine agility, where dogs running alongside their owners are sent over, under, and through a series of obstacles while competing for the best time in a handful of categories divided by the height. The sport started as an audience-pleasing exhibition before the Best in Show finals of the prestigious Crufts dog show and is based on the equine sport of show jumping.

Flyball is another relatively new sport, a relay race in which a dog runs over a series of low obstacles, hits a launcher with his paws, grabs the tennis ball that pops up, and runs back over the obstacle. The fastest team wins after rounds

of team-versus-team competition, with the fastest team from each heat advancing toward the final. Flyball was invented for an appearance on *The Tonight Show*.

The most recent of the newer sports is generically referred to as "dancing with your dog." Handlers teach their dogs a series of movements—the more creative, the better—and then choreograph, working with their dogs in a finished routine set to music, sometimes with both owner and dog in costume. The results are entertaining and often jaw-dropping in their complexity. This sport, too, started as a prefinals demonstration at Crufts.

The new dog sports differ from the traditional ones in a couple of ways: First, they're not based on any useful skill that dogs once did for their keep. Second, most are open to all breeds and mixes, instead of being limited to a group of breeds, such as retriever trials for water dogs, or "go to ground" competitions for terriers.

The love of telegenic "extreme" sports has even more new canine sports gaining competitors and audiences. These events include dock diving (jumping for distance or height into a long swimming pool) and high-jumping (the record is five feet, six inches, held by a Greyhound named Cindy).

An out-of-work attack dog

ACCORDING TO THE BOOK, *Planet Dog: A Doglopedia,* more than five thousand patrol dogs—(East) German Shepherds, one presumes—were left unemployed after they were no longer needed to patrol the Eastern side of the Berlin Wall when it came down in 1989.

The problem with a black dog? People!

IN THE PET-RESCUE WORLD, they're BBDs—big, black dogs—and no matter how nice they are, there are always more of them than there are people willing to adopt them. And nobody really knows why.

But this unreasonable dislike of dogs of the "wrong color" is nothing new. In both European and Asian folk mythology, there are legends of supernatural black hounds and of danger in the night.

By night or by day, though, the big, black dogs wagging their tails in the shelters aren't any more dangerous than their lighter-colored relatives. That's why a handful of rescue groups has formed just to counter the myths and find good homes for these dogs of a darker color. If you're looking for a good pet, don't rule out these dogs!

When the game changes, so do the dogs

T HE INTRODUCTION OF GUNS changed the way people hunted and also led to a change in the kind of dogs with which they hunted. (It's no coincidence that in the United Kingdom, the kennel-club category with these dogs in it—pointers, retrievers, and spaniels—is called the Gundog Group. The American Kennel Club prefers the less-descriptive Sporting Group designation.)

B.G. (before guns), hounds were used to run down prey. With guns offering hunters the luxury of killing at a distance, the work required dogs who could point to the location of game without disturbing the birds until the gunners were in place, "flush" the birds into the air to be shot, and then pick up the game and bring it to the hunter.

The gundogs were further developed to match the conditions of the terrain — different coats for different conditions, and swimming ability for those dogs used to hunt waterfowl.

Follow the bouncing ball

TENNIS BALLS ARE SO POPULAR with dogs that many of those sold never see a court—they go straight to the dogs. In fact, some "tennis" balls are designed with dogs in mind, in decidedly nonregulation sizes and colors, and in super-tough materials designed to make it more difficult to pop the cover off or pierce the exterior and render a ball bounceless.

These popular playthings are not without risk, though. Veterinarians warn that tennis balls should be used for supervised retrieving play only, and they should never be used as chew toys. That's because a dog can compress the ball, which can then pop open in the back of the mouth, cutting off the air supply.

When used with all due caution, though, there's probably nothing more popular among dogs than tennis balls. And nothing has inspired more related products, including pet toys that fling balls as in jai alai, drive them like golf balls, and shoot them out as in a batting cage.

According to the *Guinness Book of World Records,* a Dallas, Texas, golden retriever named Augie holds the record for the most tennis balls held in the mouth at one time: five.

Products for preventing dogs from pulling

THE BASIC DOG COLLAR has been around seemingly as long as dogs have, but in recent years inventors have been very busy trying to come up with novel ways to making walking the dog an easier activity on both ends of the leash.

The two most notable new products in this regard are the head halter and the front-clip harness. Both have gotten rave reviews from trainers and dog owners alike.

The head halter is the older of the two. It's based on a piece of equipment as old as the dog collar: an equine head halter. See, a horse is too large and strong to be controlled by a collar, so horse-handlers figured out long ago that if you can control a horse's head, the body will follow.

A couple decades ago, that principle was applied to dogs. It works not only because of the "body follows the head" rule, but also because the collar applies the same pressure as a mom dog does when she wants a pup's attention.

The head halters are popular, but some dogs hate them, even if properly introduced. Plus, some owners don't like the appearance that their dog's wearing a muzzle—it makes a good-natured dog look "mean." So inventors came up with the front-clip harness.

It's exactly as described: a harness in which the leash clips in the front of the chest, instead of on top of the back between the shoulder blades. This design uses the dog's own forward momentum to control pulling, and the animal soon learns not to forge ahead.

All hail the poodle!

MAKE FUN ALL YOU WANT, but few breeds over time have been as versatile a working dog as has the poodle. They've been used to hunt birds and truffles, trained to perform tricks in circuses, and have worked as service dogs to people with disabilities. They've also served as messengers in wartime and even as sled dogs (although the latter was more for show than for go). They're also routinely on top of the competition when Best in Show is named, perhaps in some small way because dog-show judges respect the difficulty of keeping a poodle in show condition.

The poodle is so popular that the breed is the

most common contributor to the ranks of the "designer dog" fad. While cockapoos (cocker-poodle mixes) have been around forever, the poodle is half of many new mixed-breed creations, including Labradoodles and Maltipoos.

Their strangest job of all? Topiary. In these competitions, dog groomers show off their skills; they are given a clean, white standard poodle and encouraged to dye and clip the dog into a work of canine art, such as a salute to St. Patrick's Day (a vision in kelly green), Stars and Stripes forever (red, white, and blue), or many other thematic creations that truly show poodles' strongest attribute of all: a sense of humor.

Royal dog became
a matter of style

FEW BREEDS ARE AS TIED to a time and place as the Borzoi is to the Art Deco movement of the early twentieth century. Formerly known as the Russian Wolfhound, this elegant breed—the favorite hound of the Russian royalty—was perhaps saved from extinction after the Russian Revolution by its striking good looks, which inspired all manner of decorative elements, from hood ornaments to mantelpiece clocks and jewelry.

Viagra for dogs: it's not what you think

VIAGRA (SILDENAFIL) IS USED for more than what it's most famous for. In both humans and canines, the drug is prescribed for severe pulmonary hypertension, or high pressures in the lung vessels. The disease is physically debilitating, and many affected dogs are unable to walk across the room without collapsing. Once they receive the proper dose of Viagra, however, these dogs can take short, daily walks with their owners and return to a more normal quality of life.

So if you overhear Viagra being dispensed by your veterinarian, you'll know it's more likely for a heart condition than for "performance"—especially in a neutered dog!

Drink up!

THE AVERAGE DAILY WATER intake for a dog is about three ounces for every five pounds of body weight, so a twenty-five-pound dog would drink about a pint of water per day under average conditions. The amount goes up if the weather is hot, the dog is exercising, or both.

Depending on whether a pet eats canned or dry food, up to half of the pet's daily water consumption can come from food.

Dogs drink a lot of water, not only because they need it for normal bodily functioning, but also to create moist nasal mucous to help them with their keen sense of smell.

"Dog years": an idea that doesn't compute

THE IDEA THAT EACH YEAR of a dog's life equals seven human ones isn't accurate—but the formulas to replace that easy-to-remember computation are too complicated to ever really catch on.

The first eight months of a dog's life equal thirteen years in human terms—birth to puberty, in other words. At one year, a dog's a teenager, equivalent to an eighteen-year-old human, with a little filling out still to do. After the age of two, when a dog's about twenty-one in human terms, every dog year equals approximately five human ones.

These are ballpark estimates, of course,

because the fact is that dogs age at very different rates. Small dogs may hit puberty at five months, while some larger ones may be more than a year and a half old before a female comes into heat for the first time.

So when is a dog "old"? Giant breeds such as Great Danes are senior citizens at six; a Labrador Retriever may be considered old at eight. A little dog like the Pomeranian, however, could behave like a healthy adult well into her teens.

Counting the breeds

I T'S IMPOSSIBLE TO SAY with absolute certainty how many breeds of dogs there are in the world. Different registration bodies recognize some breeds but not others, and sometimes they count as two or more breeds what other organizations count as varieties of the same breed. And then there's a case to be made that new breeds are being created all the time.

In round figures, there are more than 350 breeds worldwide. In North America, the American Kennel Club recognizes 155 breeds; the Canadian Kennel Club, 174. In the United Kingdom, the Kennel Club puts their count at 207. The FCI (Fédération Cynologique Internationale), a worldwide organization based in Belgium, recognizes 335.

For the sake of argument, a breed is defined as breeding "true," with breed qualities — curly hair, thick tail, love of water, etc. — "fixed" through selective breeding. You can mate one member of a breed to another of the same breed and get more members of that breed. Pug plus Pug equals more Pugs, in other words.

The new "designer dogs" are not considered breeds, by the way, because they don't breed true. By definition, each is created from the mating of dogs from two different breeds. A Pug plus a Beagle equals a Puggle, for example, but a Puggle plus a Puggle won't necessarily equal a dog who looks like the result of a Pug-Beagle mix.

Not that it matters to anyone who loves his dog, no matter the breeding.

Short legs for a reason

THE DOG BREEDS BEST KNOWN for having short legs are probably the Dachshund (which comes in two sizes and smooth, long-haired and wire coats) and the Corgi (which comes in two varieties: the tailless Pembroke and the Cardigan). These breeds were bred to be short-legged because of the work they were developed to do, which is different in each case.

The Dachshund was developed to "go to ground"—head underground and dig—after animals considered to be pests, primarily badgers. (Dachshund is German for "badger dog.") The short legs made it possible to fit down holes after prey. The front legs are a sort of preindustrial Rototiller, capable of moving lots of dirt. Although today's Dachshunds are almost all pets, a few of them still hunt, either for real or in trials that mimic hunting conditions, except that no prey animals are hurt.

Corgis are short for a different reason. They're herding breeds, and their style of moving cattle is to drive them forward by pushing them from behind. Cattle don't much like being bothered by pesky dogs, though, and are prone to kicking at whatever's annoying them. Those kicks for the most part sail right over the heads of the short-legged Corgis.

Styles change, even in the dogs

WHEN THE AMERICAN KENNEL Club started keeping track of the popularity of breeds, the first number one dog was an all-American favorite: The Boston Terrier. Since then, five breeds have dominated the top spot:

- The German Shepherd (thank you, Rin Tin Tin!), starting in 1925
- The Cocker Spaniel, starting in 1936
- The Beagle, starting in 1953
- The Poodle, starting in 1960
- The Cocker Spaniel (again), starting in 1983
- The Labrador Retriever, starting in 1991

The Poodle has had the longest single run at the top of the charts, but the breed also has a bit of an advantage. Toy, Miniature, and Standard Poodles all count for the total, even though the three sizes are shown as different breeds—and in the case of the Toy Poodle, in an entirely different breed group!

The Labrador Retriever's popularity is widespread. In 2005, the breed was number one in the United States, Canada, and the United Kingdom.

Dogs and cats together—a world gone mad!

WHILE THE IDEA of dogs and cats at war with each other is a comedic staple, in fact 47 percent of people who share their homes with a cat also have a dog. These pets get along to varying degrees, from out-and-out loathing to familial affection. If properly (as in slowly, at the animals' own speed) introduced, dogs and cats usually at least tolerate each other well.

More households have dogs, by the way, but there are more pet cats in the United States. How is that possible? More dogs are "only children," while the average number of cats kept in the average household has increased to nearly 2.5. That figure more reflects the ease of caring for a cat—or the perception of easy care—than the interest cats have in sharing space. In fact, dogs would much rather have canine companionship than your average cat would like a feline housemate. That's because dogs prefer more of a social structure than cats generally do.

For many families, though, the cat and dog do more than tolerate each other—the cross-species affection is quite obvious.

Although there are always exceptions to every rule, some breeds and their mixes may not enjoy a feline companion as much as others do. Breeds with high prey drive—such as terriers, hounds, and some Northern breeds, such as Huskies— may see cats more as lunch than as family without a great deal of training and careful supervision.

When you have a cat and are considering a

purebred dog, consider a breed less likely to be a problem with feline family members. Or adopt an adult, and ask the shelter or rescue group if the dog you're considering has been "cat-tested" for safety.

The big business
of feeding dogs

I N 1950, THE PET-FOOD business (which was mostly for dogs) was a $200 million industry. By 2007, it was $16.1 billion (for all pets).

Helping humans,
on command

THE IDEA OF TRAINING a dog to help humans with disabilities or chronic illnesses has come a long way. The visually impaired have dogs to see dangers, and the hearing impaired have dogs who alert them to sounds. Recently, dogs have been trained to help people with diabetes monitor their blood sugar or to alert a person with epilepsy when a seizure is coming.

Other dogs are routinely trained to help people who use wheelchairs. Dogs such as those trained by Canine Companions for Independence are taught forty helpful behaviors, from turning lights on and off to picking up dropped items to pulling a wheelchair forward.

There's seemingly no limit to the number of ways dogs have helped and will continue to help people!

Swimming? For some dogs, it's more like sinking

WHILE SOME DOGS seem almost as at home in the water as a seal, other dogs don't like getting their feet wet. And some breeds can't swim at all.

Any list of the water hounds would have to include the Retrievers, including the Labrador and Golden, perennially two of the most popular breeds worldwide. But other dogs don't mind getting wet, especially when it gets hot. Working Border Collies, for example, head for the livestock water troughs for a good soaking, and they are often enthusiastic retrievers on land or in water.

Front-heavy breeds such as Bulldogs tend to

sink like stones in the water, though, which is why people who breed or rescue these dogs advise new owners to make sure that if they have a pool, there's a fence around it or a system that sounds a warning when a child or dog falls in.

Drowning isn't just for dogs who aren't designed for swimming, though. Even water dogs can get themselves into trouble if overly tired or in dangerous currents. It's always up to the owner to make sure conditions are safe for pets.

If only my mate

IN A SURVEY SPONSORED by the American Kennel Club, an overwhelming majority of dog lovers (90 percent) said their dogs had personality traits that would be ideal in a spouse.

For women, that meant always being in a good mood, always being willing to cuddle, and never complaining about what's on the dinner menu. Men like dogs who are happy to hang around the house, are always glad to see them, and don't mind how often sports are on the TV.

How important are these traits? A full two-thirds of single dog owners said they wouldn't consider dating someone who didn't like their pet.

Ahhhh . . . that's the spot

DOGS PUMP THEIR LEGS when you hit that "special spot" because of an instinctive reaction to skin irritations such as fleas. If nerve endings detect something annoying the skin, the dog's leg will come up to scratch off the pest, most notably near the base of the tail, the upper flanks, or on the belly—all places fleas love to congregate, not coincidentally.

The "scratch reflex" is so predictable that veterinarians will use it to help with their diagnoses when spinal damage is suspected.

The detective is a dog

THE WORD "SLEUTH" has a canine origin. Dogs who were the ancestors of the breed now known as the Bloodhound were so good at tracking that they were also called Slot Hounds, from the Old Norse word "sloth," to track. Over time, this became "sleuth," popular shorthand for anyone involved in sniffing out crime.

What a yawning dog is telling you

WHEN DOGS YAWN, it's not because they're tired or bored. A yawn increases the flow of oxygen and boosts the heart rate— actions that give the brain a good goosing. A yawn can prepare the body for action—as in the yawning of a keynote speaker waiting for her introduction or a quarterback waiting to get back onto the field. Yawning can also be a way to relax.

Dogs yawn both to charge themselves up and to calm themselves down. It depends on the situation. If you go to a canine agility competition, you'll often spot dogs yawning at the starting line while waiting for the signal to explode

across the line to the first obstacle. They're ready to run, and the yawn expresses that stress and excitement. In the waiting room of a veterinary hospital, you'll often see dogs yawning, too—a sure sign that they're stressed and trying to calm themselves.

In training classes, dogs will often yawn—and owners will often interpret this as a sign that the dog is bored. Not so. The dog who's yawning in obedience class is more likely stressed than bored, either from nervousness or from wanting to please you but not yet understanding how.

Just as in humans, yawning can be contagious in dogs. If you catch your dog's attention and yawn, you may well get a yawn back. Some experienced dog handlers actually use this to their advantage, encouraging their dogs to yawn as a way to get them either focused or relaxed.

Gromit the dog . . .
was once a cat

GROMIT, THE FAITHFUL DOG in the popular Wallace and Gromit movies, was originally supposed to be a cat. Creator Nick Parks switched to a dog when he realized a canine figure would be easier to make in clay than would a feline.

Down? Don't want to!

TEACHING A DOG TO LIE down on command can be a bit of a struggle because many times a dog owner doesn't understand what "down" means to a dog.

What we think of as simply laying down is an admission of submission to a dog. Many dogs won't have any problem with that at all: they're happy with you in charge. But a dog with a more assertive personality won't willingly grant you superior status and will not be keen to lie down when you ask.

The whole "down" thing has been pretty controversial in the dog-training world in recent years, where some trainers take the idea even further, advocating rolling an aggressive dog over and pinning him to show him who's boss. The majority thinking these days is that forcing a down or a rollover with an assertive dog is a good way to get bitten, and it isn't necessary with a dog who is a happy follower, not a leader.

"Where's my statue"

IN NEW YORK'S Central Park is a statue of Balto, the sled dog who led the way into the pre-state Alaskan town of Nome with life-saving medicine in 1925. The dog who should at least be given equal credit for the task was a husky named Togo. He led his team 274 miles, but Balto led his team the last 55 miles—and got all the glory. At the time, Balto's canine celebrity was such that perhaps only the movie star Rin Tin Tin had more name recognition.

In all, some 20 mushers and 150 sled dogs—some of whom lost their lives in the effort—covered the 674 miles. That 1925 event is among the mushing traditions commemorated annually with the Iditarod sled dog race, which runs a thousand miles from Anchorage to Nome.

Mom was
very tired indeed

THE LARGEST LITTER of dogs ever recorded was born in 2005. A Neapolitan mastiff named Tia gave birth by Cesarean section to twenty-four puppies in the United Kingdom. Four of the little ones died not long after birth, but the record still held. Three dogs had previously given birth to litters of twenty-three.

Tia's owners, by the way, were expecting about ten puppies.

The diseases of dogs— and people

THERE'S A REASON rabies shots are required by law—vaccinating pets protects people from this deadly disease. Worldwide, rabies kills more than 55,000 people per year. Rabies may be the most serious thing you could possibly get from your dog, but it's not the only thing.

The nasty list of things you don't want to catch (or have your dog sick from) includes salmonella, leptospirosis, and campylobacteriosis, to name three that are bacterial in nature. Parasites can also be shared, including tapeworm, hookworm, roundworm, Lyme disease, and giardia. And then there's ringworm, which is really a fungus.

Dogs aren't the only sources of these diseases and parasites. Rabies is more prevalent in wild animals than in pets. And a case of salmonella can come from contaminated food or improper food handling at home.

Keeping dogs — and all your pets — healthy will go a long way to keeping human family members healthy, too.

A dog's world
is not black and white

DOGS DO SEE COLORS, but not as many as we can see. And the colors they see aren't as rich, either. If you throw a tennis ball in the grass, the yellow color makes it easier for you to see against the green. Not so for your dog, who could find a blue tennis ball much more easily if she had to use her eyes to find it.

Which she won't, since she'll probably sniff it out before she sees it.

Sorry, still need those nail clippers

UNLESS A DOG IS BEING walked all day long, the abrasive action of a concrete sidewalk isn't enough to wear down a dog's nails. Ideally, those nails will be given a little trim on a weekly basis, which isn't that hard to do once a pet's conditioned to understand that frequent, minor trims won't hurt and are followed by praise, petting, and treats.

Dogs learn to hate nail-trimming, though, when it's done once in a blue moon and usually involves the accidental and painful opening of the blood vessel in the nail. When a dog's nails are very long, it's usually better to ask your veterinarian to do the initial cutting and demonstrate proper follow-up care.

The most forgotten nails are the dewclaws, the ones higher up on the legs that don't hit the ground at all. These nails are sometimes so neglected that they'll grow all the way back around and dig into the flesh of the leg.

Not all dogs have dewclaws, by the way. Some are born without them, and some have them removed in the first few days after birth. When dewclaws are loose and floppy, they're called nonarticulated, and these are more prone to injury. Articulated dewclaws sit tight on the leg and are less likely to catch on things and be injured.

The Great Pyrenees is one of the few breeds required to have dewclaws—and lots of them. Double dewclaws are required on the rear feet.

Little dogs, big popularity

THE LABRADOR RETRIEVER may be the most popular single breed of dog, but small dogs have made big gains in popularity in recent years. In the 1940s, the American Kennel Club reported that one in five registered dogs came from the Toy Group. Today, it's closer to a third.

Factor in those couple of little dogs who can be found in most of the other groups (such as the Dachshunds in the Hound Group or the Bichon Frise and Lhasa Apso in the Non-Sporting Group) and all the little dogs in the Terrier Group (with more than a dozen and a half relatively small breeds), and you can make the case that small dogs totally rule.

Which came first: the wiener or the wiener dog?

A COMMON NICKNAME for the Dachshund is "wiener dog," a resemblance that's played up with common costumes for these dogs shaped like buns—complete with mustard and catsup around the back!

But the sausage creation on a bun we call the "hot dog" was probably named after its resemblance to the dog, not the other way around. The term either came from baseball or the dorms at Yale around the turn of the last century, and either was a comment on the sausage's resemblance to the Dachshund or referred (kiddingly, one assumes) to the presumed source of the meat.

The people who make hot dogs prefer the baseball story, for obvious reasons.

Lapping . . . or ladling?

WHEN BRINGING WATER into the mouth, a dog's tongue is curled backward, forming a kind of a ladle. Because the curl is almost flat across, instead of cup-shaped, much of the water spills out from the sides before the dog can get it into his mouth. This is why about half the water a dog tries to drink ends up back in the bowl or on the floor. That explains the mess!

Seems pretty inefficient, but a midsize dog can manage to slurp down a cup of water in about fifteen seconds.

Tag, you're it!

THE BEST WAY TO CATCH the family dog on the lam (assuming he won't come when called) is to run *away* from him. Run toward your dog, and he'll keep running. Run away, and many dogs will naturally follow. Once your dog is moving in the right direction, you can often crouch down and open your arms, and your dog will get close enough to catch.

Never punish your dog for coming to you, even if you spent an hour trying to catch him. If you do, you'll pretty soon guarantee your dog will keep running next time.

If ever faced with an emergency—like an oncoming car—and your dog won't come, use the command to sit. Many dogs don't like to come (as in, come back inside from having fun, come leave the dog park, come get your bath) because of the negative connotation. But dogs have mostly positive experiences with sit (sit to get a leash on for a walk, sit for treats) and will do it readily.

One Borzoi, two Borzoi, three Borzoi

W HAT DO YOU GET WHEN you have two of the breed sometimes known as a Russian Wolfhound? Two Borzois or two Borzoi?

Webster's might disagree, but fanciers of many breeds insist on some decidedly nonstandard plural forms for their mostly foreign breeds. No matter how many Borzoi you have, for example, fanciers say to forget the "s." Some other breeds and their unusual plural forms include: Keeshond (Keeshonden), Komondor (Komondorok), Kuvasz (Kuvaszok), and Puli (Pulik).

Truth in advertising

THE NAMES OF SOME DOG breeds are more descriptive than others, even if we English speakers don't know it. For example, schnauzer is German for "whiskered snout," which is certainly appropriate for this handsome breed's trademark beard, without which few would recognize him. The name of the Bichon Frise is derived from descriptive words for "short beard" and "with curly hair," which suits this fluffy little charmer to a tee.

Other descriptive breed names are not flattering and were discarded along with way. Our favorite of these has to be one of the original names of the Bouvier des Flanders (literally, "dog of Flanders"): The Vuilbaard, which means "dirty beard." "Bouvier" certainly sounds a lot classier!

Who ever heard of Spratt's

OF THE TWO OLDEST BRANDS of dog food, only one has any name recognition today: Milk Bone, which was originally called Bennett's Milk-Bone Dog and Puppy Foods, and was among the first to be sold in small, convenient boxes. The main competition at the time—the early twentieth century—was the British company, Spratt's. Both offered what would now be thought of as a "biscuit"—a dry food blending animal protein, grains, and fats.

Canned food in the early days was largely horsemeat, which was widely available because of the sudden unemployment of horses displaced by the internal combustion engine. Then as now, the slaughter of horses was intensely loathed by many Americans, but widely accepted by Europeans. Ken-L Ration was founded by a horse trader, who found the early going pretty tough. By the second half of the century, the brand was well-established and expanded beyond its origins, and was known among other things for sponsoring a Dog Hero of the Year award and for the advertising jingle every baby boomer remembers, "My dog's better than your dog/my dog's better than yours . . . "

The very name Ken-L Ration speaks volumes about how different the relationship with dogs was perceived at the time. Today, dogs sleep on the bed, not in a kennel or doghouse. And the word "ration," with its suggestion of limitations, just wouldn't suit!

Dogs eat grass because . . . they like to

MOST PEOPLE BELIEVE that dogs chew on grass because of an upset tummy. While that may factor into the urge to graze on some occasions, it's more likely dogs eat grass simply because they like to. The fiber probably helps with digestion, too.

Dogs are predators, which means that their ancestors survived by eating meat. In the wild, however, it's not all cuts of juicy sirloin, but the entire animal—including the vegetation found in the stomachs of herbivores.

Or maybe dogs eat grass just because it tastes good or they like the feel of grass augering down their indiscriminate palate. Many dogs show a distinct preference for tender shoots, especially those glossy with morning dew or damp from a cooling shower.

So don't assume "tummy ache" when your dog grazes. He may just be a bit of an omnivorous gourmet, seeking out the best of the available vegetation.

And it's not just grass, either. Many dogs adore nibbling on all manner of plant treats, to the extent that many veterinarians recommend substituting baby carrots or thawed frozen green beans for the treats of pudgy dogs—and the dogs love them!

Veterinarians get specialized

JUST AS IN HUMAN MEDICINE, in veterinary medicine you'll find an increasing number of specialists. They're called "boarded" because their over-and-above credentials are given by a governing board after the veterinarian passes additional requirements in study (passing a test), practice (serving a residency), or both.

Those veterinarians who earn specialist certification will list extra credentials after their degree in veterinarian medicine. For example, after a DVM (doctor of veterinary medicine) you'll find

Diplomate (sometimes abbreviated as Dip or just D) and the initials of the certifying body, such as the American College of Veterinary Internal Medicine.

A handful of the specialties related to the care of dogs includes cardiology, dermatology, dentistry, oncology, and surgery.

Cure for the yellow lawn blues

FEMALE DOGS GET THE RAP for yellow spots on the lawn, but in fact there's nothing particularly different between the urine of male and female dogs as far as lawns are concerned. It's the action that's the difference: females squat and release most of their urine at once, while males lift and tend to divide their yellow gift among a number of vertical surfaces.

The best way to prevent yellow spots is to teach your dog to potty in a place that cannot be damaged. If that's not possible, flushing the area where urine was left with clean water will help to diminish the destruction.

It's commonly believed that urine burns the lawn; in fact, the liquid acts as a powerful nitrogen-based fertilizer, making the grass grow itself to death.

Barking dog?
Look out!

THE OLD ADAGE "a barking dog won't bite" isn't true: dogs who bark may bite as well. Dogs will even bite while wagging their tails.

Tax that tail

THE CREATIVE WAYS government finds to levy taxes may factor into the history of why some dogs started having their tails soon after birth.

Ear cropping (to create an upright ear) and tail docking (to make a stubby tail) are thought to have started with the Romans, who believed in the practice for rabies prevention. In later centuries, though, working dogs were not taxed and were docked to identify them as exempt. In working terriers, the stump tail provided a useful handle for pulling a dog out of a hole when it was hunting.

Tail docking is typically done on newborn

puppies. The practice is banned in some countries and controversial in others. Even in countries where it's legal, there's argument over whether breeders should be able to dock tails or if it should be limited to veterinarians.

In the United States, tails are routinely docked by breeders or veterinarians, although the American Veterinary Medical Association has for more than a decade held the position that both ear cropping and tail docking are medically unnecessary and don't help dogs in any way.

Popularity can be a curse

THE PHENOMENON IS NOT a new one: when a breed of dog is featured in a popular movie or on TV, popularity soars. Unfortunately, many of the breeds given such bursts of fame haven't been among the easiest with which to live.

Rin Tin Tin and Lassie were among the earliest dogs to inadvertently drive demand for a breed, but the list in recent decades has been long indeed. The Dalmatian has seen waves of popularity, first in the '60s with the animated *101 Dalmatians* and again with every remake of the franchise.

The TV shows *Wishbone* and *Frasier* gave the

Parson Russell Terrier (more commonly known as the Jack Russell Terrier) a big boost, but it doesn't take a whole show to put a breed in demand.

The words "yo quiero Taco Bell," seemingly spoken by a hungry Chihuahua in ads for the fast-food chain, had everyone wanting one of the spunky little dogs.

To their credit, movie studios and TV shows these days often work with dog clubs in advance, warning people that in real life dogs rarely behave as well or as amusingly as they do on the screen.

Long, longer, longest

A BASSET HOUND named Mr. Jeffries set the record for having the longest ear flaps in the world, at 11.5 inches. The dog is notable for another reason as well. His grandfather was the Basset Hound in advertisements for the Hush Puppies brand of shoes.

Dognapping
of the sleepy kind

A DOG CAN SPEND more than half his life asleep—ten to thirteen hours a day—and older dogs spend even more time sleeping. Some breeds are more active than others, and outdoor dogs spend more time awake than indoor dogs.

The weather can also change a dog's sleep. Pets will tend to sleep more on cloudy days than sunny ones, and snuggle up more on cold days than warm ones.

🐾 About the Authors

Dr. Marty Becker

As a veterinarian, media personality, author, and educator, Dr. Marty Becker has become known as the "best-loved family doctor for pets."

Marty is the popular veterinary contributor to ABC-TV's *Good Morning, America* and the host of *The Pet Doctor* on PBS. He is also the coauthor (with Gina Spadafori) of the "Pet Connection," a popular feature syndicated to newspapers and websites internationally through Universal Press Syndicate. Marty has appeared on Animal Planet, and he is a frequent guest on national network and cable television, as well as radio shows. He has been interviewed for countless magazine and newspaper articles on pets and their care.

Marty is an adjunct professor at his alma mater, Washington State University College of Veterinary Medicine, and at the Colorado State University College of Veterinary Medicine. Additionally, he has lectured at every veterinary school in the United States and been named Companion Animal Veterinarian of the Year by the Delta Society and the American Veterinary Medical Association.

Marty is coauthor of the fastest-selling pet book in history, *Chicken Soup for the Pet Lover's Soul,* and is either sole author or coauthor of other top-selling books, including other animal books in the *Chicken Soup* line, *The Healing Power of Pets: Harnessing the Amazing Ability of Pets to Make and Keep People Happy and Healthy,* and *Fitness*

Unleashed! A Dog and Owner's Guide to Losing Weight and Gaining Health Together!

With Gina Spadafori, he has authored *Why Do Dogs Drink Out of the Toilet? 101 of the Most Perplexing Questions Answered About Canine Conundrums, Medical Mysteries and Befuddling Behaviors* (a *New York Times* bestseller) and *Why Do Cats Always Land on Their Feet? 101 of the Most Perplexing Questions Answered About Feline Unfathomable, Medical Mysteries, and Befuddling Behaviors*. The pair collaborated with Teresa Becker and Audrey Pavia on *Why Do Horses Sleep Standing Up? 101 of the Most Perplexing Questions Answered About Equine Enigmas, Medical Mysteries, and Befuddling Behaviors*.

Marty devotes his life to his family, which includes his beloved wife, Teresa, daughter, Mikkel, and son, Lex, along with all the furry family members on the Beckers' Almost Heaven Ranch in northern Idaho.

Gina Spadafori

Gina Spadafori has been blessed with the opportunity to combine two of her dearest loves—animals and words—into a career writing about animals. Since 1984, she has written an award-winning weekly column on pets and their care.

Gina has served on the boards of directors of both the Cat Writers Association (CWA) and the Dog Writers Association of America (DWAA). She has won the DWAA's Maxwell Medallion for the best newspaper column, and her column has also been honored with a certificate of excellence by the CWA. The first edition of her top-selling book, *Dogs for Dummies,* was given the President's Award for the best writing on dogs and the Maxwell Medallion for the best general reference work, both by the DWAA.

In addition to *Dogs for Dummies* and the books written with Dr. Becker, Gina has coauthored other award-winning books. Along with Dr. Paul D. Pion, a top veterinary cardiologist, she was given the CWA's awards for the best work on feline nutrition, best work on feline behavior, and best work on responsible cat care for the top-selling *Cats for Dummies.* The book was also named one of the hundred best feline moments in the twentieth century by *Cat Fancy* magazine. With internationally recognized avian specialist Dr. Brian L. Speer, Gina has also written *Birds for Dummies,* one of the best-selling books on pet birds ever written. Her books have been translated into many languages, including French, Serbian, Danish, Japanese, and Russian.

Gina has also headed one of the first and largest online pet-care sites, the Pet Care Forum, America Online's founding source of pet-care information.

Gina lives in northern California in a decidedly multispecies home.

Index

"A Bold Bluff," 43
Akita, 27, 88
Alaskan Malamute, 58
American Australian Shepherd, 105
American Dingo, 58
American Eskimo Dog, 58
American Foxhound, 58
American Kennel Club, 18, 87, 123, 136, 141, 151, 168
American Staffordshire Terrier, 58
American Veterinary Medical Association, 188
American Water Spaniel, 58
Annie!, 92
art depicting dogs, 42
Ashley Whippet, 116
Australian Cattle Dogs, 97
Australian Shepherd, 58

Balto, 160
Barney, 24
Basset Hound, 191
Beagle, 26, 84, 141
Bergamasco, 60
Berlin Wall, 120
Bichon Frise, 175
Bible, 68
biting behavior, 186
black dogs, 121–122
blood transfusions, 48–50
Bloodhound, *76–77*, 82, 153
Bluey, 97
body temperature, 2
Border Terrier, 66
Borzoi, 131, 174
Boston Terrier, 58
Bouvier des Flanders, 25, 176
Boxer, 36
Boykin Spaniel, 58
breeding, 95, 109–110, 136
Briard, 67

Britain's Kennel Club, 12
Bulldog, 36, 149–150
Bush, George H.W., 24
Bush, George W., 24
Byrd, Richard, 40

Canadian Kennel Club, 136
cancer sniffing, 82
Canine Companions for Independence, 147–148
cat cohabitation, 143–144
Catahoula Leopard Dog, 58
Cavalier King Charles Spaniel, 13, 25
Central Park, 160
chemical sniffing, 82
Chesapeake Bay Retriever, 58
Chihuahua, 20, 66, 190
Chinese Shar-Pei, 18
Chow Chow, 18–19, 88
Civil War, 8
Cocker Spaniel, 32–34, 141
Collie, 98–100, 149
Coolidge, Calvin, 100
Coolidge, Cassius Marcellus, 42
Coonhounds, 58
Corgi, 139
cropping ears, 187
Crufts, 104–105, 117

Dachshund, 139–140, 168, 169–170
Dalmatian, 66, 189
Dandie Dinmont Terrier, 14
digging behavior, 111–112
Doberman, Louis, 12
Doberman, 12, 88, 129
dog food, 146, 177–178
dog sports, 116–119
dog tags, *7*
dog walking, 127–128
"dog years," 134–135
"Dogs Playing Poker," 42

drinking, 133, 171
drug sniffing, 80

English Cocker Spaniel, 34
English Mastiff, 22
English Terrier, 15
English Toy Spaniel, 13
explosive sniffing, 81
eyesight, 165

Fala, 24
Federation Cynologique
    Internationale, 136–137
fleas, 53–54
flyball, 117–188
Fox Terrier, 40
foxhound, 23
Frasier, 189
Fuchsl, 16
fur, 60–62

German Shepherd, 69, 82, 88, 120, 141
Gibson, 20
Golden Retriever, 149
Gordon Setter, 14
grass, eating, 179–180
grass, yellowing, 184–185
Great Dane, 20, 66, 135
Great Pyrenees, 168
Greyhound, 68, 95
Gromit, 157
Guest, Christopher, 87
Guy Mannering, 14

Hammett, Dashiell, 29
heart rate, 1–2
Heaven Sent Brady, 20
height, 20
Hitler, Adolf, 15–16
"Hound Dog," 10
"(How Much Is) That Doggie in
    the Window?" 10
hunting dogs, 123–124
Hush Puppies, 191
Huskies, 112, 144

Iditarod, 161
Igloo, 40

Indiana Jones, 46
insect sniffing, 81
International Society of Animal
    License Collectors, 9
Irish Wolfhound, 20

Jack Russell Terrier, 12, 190
Johnson, Lyndon Baines, 26

Kamikaze-Go (*also* Kami), 27–28
Kashwitna, 90
Keeshond, 174
Keller, Helen, 27
Ken-L Ration, 178
Kennel Club (UK), 136
Kenzan-Go (*also* Go-Go), 28
King Charles Spaniel, 13
Knight, Eric, 99
Komondor, 60, 174
Kuvasz, 174

Labrador Retriever, 59, 82, 135,
    141–142, 149, 168
Lad: A Dog, 98
Lady and the Tramp, 34
Laika, 39
Landseer, Edwin, 102
Lassie, 29, 98, 99
"Last Will and Testament of
    Silverdeme Emblem," 6
lawsuits, 88
Lucas, George, 46
Lucky, 25

Malamute, 112
"man's best friend," 4
Mastiff, 95, 162
Milk Bone, 177
Millie, 24
Miniature Schnauzer, 29
Miss Beazley, 24
mold sniffing, 81
muzzle, 127
My Own Brucie, 34

nail trimming, 166–167
names, 30
neutering, 51–52

Newfoundland, 59
nose temperature, 78–79
Nova Scotia Duck Tolling
    Retriever, 59

Old Drum, 4
101 Dalmatians, 189
O'Neill, Eugene, 6
os penis, 108

Page, Patti, 10
panting, 106–107
parasites, 163
Parson Russell Terrier, 12
Pharaoh Hound, 96
photographing dogs, 72–73
Pit Bull Terriers, 88, 89
Planet Dog: A Doglopedia, 120
Pomeranian, 135
Poodles, 61–62, 129–130, 141–142
Presa Canario, 88
Presley, Elvis, 10
Prudence Prim, 100
Pug, 36
Puli, 174
pulmonary hypertension, 132

Queensland Heelers, 97

rabies, 56, 163
Reagan, Nancy, 25
Reagan, Ronald W., 25, 29
Rex (Reagan's dog), 25
Rin Tin Tin, 69, 141
Rob Roy, 100
Roosevelt, Franklin Delano, 24
Rottweiler, 66, 88
Russell, John, 12
Russian Wolfhound, 131

Saint Bernard, 14, 90, 102
salmonella, 163–164
Schnauzer, 175
Scottish terrier, 24
"scratch reflex," 152
Shakespeare, 35
Shar-Pei, 1970
Sirius,

sled dogs, 44
sleeping, 192
spaying, 51–52
Spielberg, Stephen, 46
Spratt's, 177
Springer Spaniel, 24
Sputnik 2, 39
Susitna, 90
swimming, 149–150

tail docking, 187–188
teeth, 63
Terriers, 112, 168
Tempest, The, 35
tennis balls, 125–126
Terhune, Albert Payson, 98
Thin Man, The, 29
Thrapthon Association for the
    Prevention of Felons, 77
Three Dog Night, 10
Tonight Show, The, 118
Toy Fox Terrier, 58
training, 147–148, 158–159
Truman, Harry S, 23

vaccinations, 55–56, 163
Vest, George Graham, 4, 6
veterinarian specialty, 182–183
Viagra, 132

Walter Scott, Sir, 14
Washington, George, 23
"Waterloo," 43
Westminster Kennel Club, 34,
    86–87
Wire Fox Terrier, 29
Wishbone, 189
wookies, 46
working dogs, 113–114
World War I, 8, 15, 69
World War II, 24
world's largest litter, 162
World's Oldest Dog, 97
World's Strongest Dog, 90

yawning, 154–156

Zorba de la-Susa, 22